Welcome to your next 31 Days!
Mothers, single, married & other

As a mother we experience a myriad of emotion on any given day; the feelings can begin in joy and at the drop of a hat turn into grief, anger, confusion, or despair.

No matter what the feeling of the moment may be, they are all rooted in love and the focus is that of the children that we nurture.

I encourage a positive attitude based on a spiritual grounding, mine is rooted in Christianity.

Rather a follower of Christ or not, over the next 31 days, allow this text to reassure and affirm you as you walk through each day being the best mother that you can be.

Welcome to your next 31 Days!

Day 4, "My kids, the best thing, I never knew I needed"

Children change you! That could be the entire affirmation for the day. As much as we fight it, as much as we deny it, being a mom, changes us. There'll be days where you question why you signed up for this job. Things have started sagging. Other parts may have stretched, there's extra weight and a perpetual state of exhaustion. You can't sleep enough when you have children and when they're small, it doesn't seem like anyone sleeps at all. They change you. They don't just change you physically, they change the way you think, act and live. Children enhance you and make you better. Think about how different your life would have been had they not

been here. Now stop smiling because you weren't marrying that actor or traveling daily throughout the year. If we're honest with ourselves, our children have grounded us. They've encouraged us to stop participating in certain activities and discouraged us from giving up. They're a chore at times but they're the best things that we never knew we

needed. Nothing encourages us like our child's hug or their poorly drafted drawing. There's no greater love than the snotty nosed kiss or your teen simply laying across the foot of your bed talking to you about their day. It is the little gestures of love that grow us and remind us why we struggle, stress and strain to make sure that there's food, a roof over their heads and clothes on their back. There is no greater love than that of a child and love changes things, more importantly, us. Continue to grow into the greatest mommy that you can be. Your child loves you for it.

Day 4, "My kids, the best thing, I never

Day 1, "I can't BUT I have to"

Nothing prepares you for motherhood, there is no text or guidebook that equips you with the knowledge needed to be a "great" mom. It's on the job training where you pick up tidbits from your environment. You practice what worked well in your home while you avoid what failed miserably. You look to those who you deem the "perfect" parent and you hope that your child at least turns out, normal. Not a criminal. Not a sociopath. Not emotionally damaged. Not a dropout. Not a teen parent. Not extremely awkward. Not this. Not that. Just, at bare minimum, "normal", whatever that is.
With no rule book or direction, you started this journey and all you know is that you must be a "great" parent.

This little person did not ask to be here. You decided, based on whatever the circumstance to bring life into this world and although you "can't", you absolutely must be the best parent that you can be. Because you made the decision to follow through and not abort this mission, you can and you will be GREAT, even on those days that you hardly feel like being a woman. There is no such thing as perfect. "Great" is subjective.
Your children judge you on the love you give and if you continually do your best, you're going to be perfect to them.

Day 1, "I can't BUT I have to"

Day 2, "If it wasn't for GOD"

Parenting is a fulltime, 365-day, 24-hour, 7 day per week job. It's required with resources, without resources. With sleep, without sleep. Sane or insane. The job must get done. No off days. No sleeping in. Little recognition. Lots of stress and sometimes lots of tears. The plan wasn't to do it alone. The idea was to have found a career, established great credit, built a home and married the man of your dreams. That was the plan. It did not work out that way.

There is no inkling of the dream job, just yet. You're still trying to figure out your purpose. Credit? There's debt and lots of it. Your rent is expensive and that Prince Charming… let's just say, no one is rescuing you from any towers any time soon. It's okay. Life rarely works out the way we plan. That's why we must look to the hills from which cometh our help and absolutely must set our sights on the things above. As you look back throughout this journey, identify those times that you absolutely thought there was no way out, yet you're sitting here reading this text. Be reminded and reassured that the same GOD that brought you through those trials will absolutely bless you continually along the way.

Remember how far you have come and keep that on your life's windshield as you continue to move forward. You can do this!
God has your back, no matter what it looks like.
He did it before and He is going to do it again! Be encouraged, mom!

Day 2, "If it wasn't for GOD"

Day 3, "More MONTH than money"

There's never enough money when kids are involved. I'm sorry, I was supposed to start out positive with a set uprooted in a false expectation. There's no such thing as sufficiency in parenting. There's no such thing because you can't plan for everything. You have no idea what surprises lie ahead on this journey.

You must be okay with this fact. Don't beat yourself up for what you can't do when you're doing the best that you can. Do not look to the left or right, comparing your circumstances to someone else.

Your road is your road, and no one can travel it or make it work like you so get used to having more month than money. No, I am not saying accept insufficiency. Always strive to do better and reach the heights that you set forth for your life. What I am saying is that for you to correct the issue, you must first accept that there is one.

Once you have done that, you can start to plan a course of attack. You can start to identify what expenses are unnecessary. You will start to identify where you can cut back. You can build a better budget and discipline yourself to follow it more carefully. You can start the investment in insurances, college funds and retirement plans with pennies on the dollar. You can hide money from yourself for rainy days. Right now, there's not enough so start planning by putting away something for the unexpected. You'll never be prepared for everything. It will often seem like there is far more month than money, but you can be in a position to attack the financial obstacles that arise. You will be in a position of preparedness so that no matter what comes up, there's a way to manage it. You got this mommy!

Day 3, "More MONTH than money"

Day 5, "Not TODAY Satan"

If one more thing goes wrong, you are going to scream! Scream! Go ahead! I won't tell! As a matter of fact, I'll scream with you! Yes! Let it out! Yell to the top of your lungs! Do you feel better? Did that obstacle leave? Probably not but at least some stress has been relieved and worse case, you made yourself laugh from the vision of your screaming uncontrollably, unless of course you actually screamed. If so, this is a judgment free zone!

As mommies, we have and will have these moments. What are our options? Run and hide? Hopefully by the time we come out, this will all have gone away or mysteriously cleared itself up. Unfortunately, that is not really an option. There are lives depending on us working through our disappointments, frustrations, and aggravations. There are lives that hang in the balance of our decisions. It's with them in mind that we must suck it up and say, "NOT today Satan!" You will not be moved! You will not be discouraged!

You understand that life never promised to be perfect and obstacles will come but you are more than a conqueror and can make it through anything. Yes, I said anything! This may be hard but it's just a distraction. Tomorrow is a new day. Take them one at a time. Mommy, you are going to be fine! This TOO shall pass!

Day 5, "Not TODAY Satan"

Day 6, "Where did THAT even come from"

Congratulations! You're pregnant! If you were anything like me this news wasn't completely shocking, but it wasn't totally welcomed either. I wasn't prepared to raise a child. I was a child, but I eventually realized what my purpose was. Your purpose as a mother is to raise this child. To rear this child. To support this child and more importantly, to love this child. Everything begins in the home. We try to blame outside influences and experiences along the way, although these things are factors, the root is formed in the home.

When your 16-year-old starts going crazy and morphs into this unrecognizable force called a teenager, you may ask, "where did that even come from?"

When your 5-year-old has a tantrum because they wanted sketchers with lights as opposed to sketchers with Velcro straps and characters, you may ask," where did that even come from?"

Truth is that our children mimic what they see before they ever mimic what we say, and it is amazing what little actions they pick up on. Mommy be the change that you want to see in your children. Some things are inevitable but if you are being the best mom you can, no matter how far that child strays, and they will stray, they'll come back to the root. The success of your children typically mirrors the way they were raised.

Day 6, "Where did THAT even come from"

Day 7," I don't know HOW but I know WHO"

But God! That's simple enough and typically the answer to who blessed us and solved that problem. It's a struggle. Parenting is hard! There's a reason why this is consistently repeated, and this text was created, parenting is not easy. There will be good days. There will be bad days. There will be mistakes. There will be milestones. The cycle of these will continue if you're parenting and the children are growing, these are inevitable. There will be lack and there will be abundance. There will be isolation. There will be times when you have mentally packed your bags and plotted, in detail, your escape.

There will be thoughts that rarely turn into actions. We both know that you are not leaving but it felt surprisingly good to walk thoroughly through that moment of abandonment. You will feel helpless. You will wonder how. All these things are normal and if you have never experienced them, it's safe to say that you're perfect. You're perfectly fooling yourself because I know better. Parenting is fluid.

There's no road map so the territory is being charted on how to raise your children as we speak. Expect to ask for help. Expect to lean on others.

Be okay with this expectation and be comfortable with walking in it. As you seek assistance in those unknown or insufficient areas, God will point you to the resources that you need to be successful.

Do not be discouraged, be prepared to ask.

Day 7," I don't know HOW but I know

Day 7," I don't know HOW but I know WHO"

But God! That's simple enough and typically the answer to who blessed us and solved that problem. It's a struggle. Parenting is hard! There's a reason why this is consistently repeated, and this text was created, parenting is not easy. There will be good days. There will be bad days. There will be mistakes. There will be milestones. The cycle of these will continue if you're parenting and the children are growing, these are inevitable. There will be lack and there will be abundance. There will be isolation. There will be times when you have mentally packed your bags and plotted, in detail, your escape.

There will be thoughts that rarely turn into actions. We both know that you are not leaving but it felt surprisingly good to walk thoroughly through that moment of abandonment. You will feel helpless. You will wonder how. All these things are normal and if you have never experienced them, it's safe to say that you're perfect. You're perfectly fooling yourself because I know better. Parenting is fluid.

There's no road map so the territory is being charted on how to raise your children as we speak. Expect to ask for help. Expect to lean on others.

Be okay with this expectation and be comfortable with walking in it. As you seek assistance in those unknown or insufficient areas, God will point you to the resources that you need to be successful.

Do not be discouraged, be prepared to ask.

Day 7," I don't know HOW but I know

Day 8, "Mother's Day"

Everyone loves Mother's Day! It's advertised months beforehand. Flowers go on sale. Jewelry is reasonably priced. Restaurants are booked well in advance and church services are at capacity. Everyone loves to celebrate their moms on this one day.

What happens the other 364 days of the year? Who's celebrating you then? The answer should be you. Mother's Day is every day, and it is critical to your sanity that you set aside time routinely to celebrate you. This is not to say that no one loves you any other day. This is not to say that you are not appreciated all 365 days. It's simply reminding you that self-care is critical to your success. You cannot pour out of an empty cup; you must take care of you. If it's just for an hour in the morning before the kids get up, soak in a tub and read a few pages of a book. If it's at lunch at work, take a walk around the building to decompress and exercise. Regardless to what the activity is and the time span, you must set aside time to celebrate yourself. Relaxation is celebration. Doing something you enjoy is celebration. Being still and quiet is celebration. If it gives you peace and brings you enjoyment, it is celebration.

Make sure that Mother's Day is not set aside for one day, take care of yourself daily.

Day 8, "Mother's Day"

Day 9, "Who are YOU"

I asked before how differently life would be if you had not become a mother, this is where your question will be answered. Think about this seriously this time but let me provide a little more context: who are you outside of your children? What were your dreams? What were your aspirations? What were your goals? How many of these things have you accomplished since you became a mother? Why haven't you accomplished these things? Think about it. Think hard and honestly about the answers to these questions. Being happy and fulfilled supports your ability to be a great parent. Remember, the definition of great is personal but your mental health, self-esteem and stability are not.

We believe that it is selfish to chase our dreams once we become moms. It's not selfish, it's a sacrifice. You can put off your dreams for a season. Sometimes it's inevitable but it's not meant to be permanent. If you don't do the things that make your heart happy, you will begin to resent the things that caused you to detour. We're individual women before we are mommies and we must nurture that individuality. This is not an excuse to become negligent in our motherly duties or to let them slip. It's a reminder that it's okay to have an identity outside of being a mom. Ask yourself, "who are you?" If the only available examples point back to your children, I charge you to dig a little deeper and identify an identity outside of them. If you don't, you'll find that once they have grown up to be the wonderful adults you are raising them to be, you'll be left without a purpose.

Day 9, "Who are YOU"

Day 10, "I've never met THESE monsters"

Have you encountered the moment when your child does something so incredibly out of character that you fail to recognize them? If it hasn't happened yet, you have a newborn. Once they start to walk and talk, it's a perpetual state of surprise and excitement. It is mostly amusing but occasionally, a cause for concern may be raised.

What do you do in these moments? How do you react? You can't return them to sender. You lost the receipt and I really don't think that they'll fit back in the box they came in. This surprise from our children is inevitable. Life is the same way. No matter what you do, something will come that will completely catch you off guard and

leave you speechless. You won't have necessarily done anything wrong and it is not something that could have been avoided. It's a guarantee of life. Mommy, it's okay. It's not your fault. Forgive yourself. Move forward. Life presents monsters in all shapes, sizes and forms. They're designed to test you and build you. There is not one obstacle that will present itself that you do not have the authority over. Remember, He did it before, He will do it again.

Sometimes difficulties arise to remind us of our help. Sometimes obstacles arise to remind us that we're still growing. Other times obstacles come to redirect us. Whatever the reasons, the monsters will come, and our help is always there.

All we have to do is ask. When you cannot do it alone, ask.

Day 10, "I've never met THESE monsters"

Day 10, "I've never met THESE monsters"

Have you encountered the moment when your child does something so incredibly out of character that you fail to recognize them? If it hasn't happened yet, you have a newborn. Once they start to walk and talk, it's a perpetual state of surprise and excitement. It is mostly amusing but occasionally, a cause for concern may be raised.

What do you do in these moments? How do you react? You can't return them to sender. You lost the receipt and I really don't think that they'll fit back in the box they came in. This surprise from our children is inevitable. Life is the same way. No matter what you do, something will come that will completely catch you off guard and

leave you speechless. You won't have necessarily done anything wrong and it is not something that could have been avoided. It's a guarantee of life. Mommy, it's okay. It's not your fault. Forgive yourself. Move forward. Life presents monsters in all shapes, sizes and forms. They're designed to test you and build you. There is not one obstacle that will present itself that you do not have the authority over. Remember, He did it before, He will do it again.

Sometimes difficulties arise to remind us of our help. Sometimes obstacles arise to remind us that we're still growing. Other times obstacles come to redirect us. Whatever the reasons, the monsters will come, and our help is always there.

All we have to do is ask. When you cannot do it alone, ask.

Day 10, "I've never met THESE monsters"

Day 11, "My GREATEST accomplishments"

When I look into the eyes of my children I am filled with pride. Although each are vastly different, they are equally great. As much as I would like to take credit for the type of adults they will become, all their success will not be because of me. There's outside influences. There's other family. And then, there's their individual drive, desire, dedication and perseverance that ultimately makes them who they are. I was just the root.

Important none the less but unfortunately, they are not my greatest accomplishments. My greatest accomplishments are those things that I solely controlled. My degrees. My business. This book. These are directly attributed to my hard work, sacrifice, drive and under my control. What are yours? Yes, we're talking about this again. I will not let you forget that you are an individual. A contributing part of society and there is something in you that the world needs. We're not all designed to perform on large

platforms and effect masses. You won't get pressure from me there. We do all have something to give and more importantly give back. We are part of someone else's village. We can mentor a teen in need. Help a child with homework. Be an example. Volunteer our time. We can each do something to effect change in the greater areas outside of our little world, our family. What do you do outside of your family to help someone else?

When you take inventory of your life, what will be your greatest accomplishment?

Day 11, "My GREATEST accomplishments"

Day 12, "THAT should have gone differently"

In parenting, how much actually goes according to plan? I'll wait while you mentally list these items that were perfectly performed. I'm certain that was quick and we're ready to move on. I'm certain because there's no such thing as perfect. The reoccurring theme in this text is that parenting is fluid. There'll be change and there'll be lots. Plans are good but they should absolutely be written in pencil with open minds because we'll discover that what was originally drafted, will change. Repeat after me, "it's okay!" Mommy, our  successes lie in our ability to move through the confusion. Maneuver around the imperfections. Navigate through the chaos. When you've mentally set aside your upcoming income tax refund to pay for that much needed family vacation to only find out that your landlord sold your building, the new owner has decided to renovate then convert to condos, so you have to move. When you worked diligently to improve your credit score because you need a vehicle and riding public transportation with children is frustrating, but you uncover that you still can't afford the vehicle you want and don't like the one that's an option. When you have landed your dream job but don't have adequate daycare, so you have to reconsider your offer. These are things that you planned for yet were usurped by unexpected obstacles. It does not by far mean that these things will not happen, it means that you must navigate through the confusion. Release the expectation that life will operate according to a plan, especially parenting.

Take the additional pressure of yourself by being okay that life must be written in pencil and sometimes things will work out differently than planned but they will work out, nonetheless.

Day 12, "THAT should have gone

Day 13, "Who's paying for THAT"

Mommy, you are!! Isn't that the expectation in your house? If something happens, mommy will take care of it. Regardless to the cost or function, if something needs to get done, mommy will put on her cape, climb up on that money tree and get things done.

Mommy and problem solver are synonymous, it is in the dictionary as such. In a perfect world, we could live up to this expectation and gladly. Unfortunately, this is unrealistic. One of the most disappointing aspects of parenting is having a child's need go unfulfilled. It's painful to tell them that you can't. You feel like you've failed when you can't. They're hurt in the moment when you can't but guess what, it's only a moment. Children do not stop loving us because we said no. Children do not trade their parents in for richer models because they were unable to meet one need. We beat ourselves up far more than that child ever will. It's our pride. We feel like we let them down. We didn't. We couldn't perform that one task and it won't be the last. Their love is endless. They appreciate that we are doing the best that we can. They see our love daily. They appreciate that. Their moment of disappointment does not affect their lifelong love. Cut yourself some slack mom, you are still a great mom when you can't.

Day 13, "Who's paying for THAT"

Day 14, "Who BROKE it"

Having to completely pour out attention, love and affection to our children is exhausting. It's not a matter of if you'll get tired, it's a matter of when. Having to routinely do anything is absolutely exhausting, being a mom is not any different. Getting tired is okay. Feeling lost at times is okay. Needing to get away is okay. All these feelings are normal.

The one time that there is a cause for sincere concern is if these are routine feelings, thoughts or you become violent. If you get to a point where your feelings are not controllable or lashing out becomes the norm, it is time to seek counseling. Something is broken and outside repair is needed. This is not anything that can be treated by rest and relaxation alone. There are feelings of anxiety and anger that must be explored so that the right help can be obtained. Please do not try to fix yourself, self- medication can cause extreme damage. You are an individual first, you must take care of you so that you can take care of your children.
If you feel broken in any area, seek help.
Helping yourself, helps your family. You can do this mommy!

Day 14, "Who BROKE it"

Day 15, "It's just Me, MYSELF & I"

There will be times when you will feel the loneliest that you have ever felt. There'll be a drastic change. The kids will leave, and you'll have failed to make plans for that weekend. Everyone will appear to have something going on in their lives but you. Whether the reason is as simple as an empty nest or as complicated as a life change, there will come a time when you will feel alone.

Your best friend in life is yourself. You should not be your only friend, but you should love yourself. You should love hanging out with you. You should love talking to you. You should be comfortable with the skin you're in and no one should love you more than you. If you love you, you will not let anyone else mistreat you. If you love you, you will not let anyone disrespect you. If you love you, you will not let any harm come to anything connected to you. Loving you is criteria for being a great mom. Healthy self-esteem is a requirement of a good life. When you feel good about you, you do better. You do better because you believe in yourself and your outlook is positive. When your outlook is positive you pass good vibes to those around you. When you pass good vibes to those around you, people like to be around you. When people like to be around you, they'll like to do things with and for you. It's reciprocity, what you sow, you reap. If you sow positivity, positivity will be returned to you. Are there exceptions? Absolutely but the norm will be that the vibes sown will be the vibes returned.

How do you feel about you?

Day 15, "It's just Me, MYSELF & I"

Day 16, "Ask your DADDY"

Ask your mommy! Isn't that the directive in every home? Mommy is the President, Dictator and Warden. Mommy has the final say. Nothing moves until mommy says so. Mommy is the tie that binds, the beginning and the end, the Alpha and the Omega. Well, that's actually God but in our homes, physically, that is absolutely mom. Yet daddy gets the big piece of chicken. Only has to look and the children straighten up. Daddy is the other most influential parent in the family, but the roles are very different. Mom, we aren't dad. No

matter how hard we try to be or attempt to bridge the gap when he is not around, we are not him. We are mommy and our power lies in that. We have vastly different gifts, strengths and weaknesses. Our different genetic makeups are not by accident but by design. Our titles are different intentionally because we provide very different things to our children. We are mutually exclusive but equally important. We are both needed. We must respect and love each other. The state of the relationship should not dictate the state of our parenting, we must keep first things first and our children are priority. You can't make anyone be anything therefore if you don't have a daddy in your child's life, a grandpa, an uncle, cousin or positive male figure is a wonderful stand in. If you do have a daddy in your child's life, the best thing that you can do for your child is to respect him. Remember, they imitate far more of what they see us do before they mimic what they hear us say. We want our great habits to carry on so that family is always first.

Day 16, "Ask your DADDY"

Day 17, "Where's YOUR daddy"

To be classified as a single mother, you must be unmarried. In a relationship or engaged still equals up to, "unmarried". "Single" means unmarried. That was most likely not the plan, but life happens. Children are born out of wedlock and relationships end. Sometimes for good reasons and other times out of sheer misunderstanding but regardless to the reason, we have found

ourselves under this label and in situations where we are wondering, "where's your daddy?" Mommy, life does not end because he is not there. The failed relationship does not mean that you are a failure. There is never any obstacle that will present itself that you do not already have victory over. If you have found yourself raising a child alone, you know that the task is hard but not impossible. You can make it. You can move on. You can be loved, and your child accepted as someone's own. There is life after the breakup. There is life after he left. It's your choice. "How is it my choice? He decided that he didn't want to be here?" You're right, now his part in your relationship is over. His part in his child's life does not have to be and your life does not have to stop. It's up to you whether that is the end. We often put so much stock in the lost relationship that we start to lose focus on what remains. There is a child that still has a need and is looking to you to fill it. There is a woman who may have been broken, that still needs to move forward. As an individual and a parent, the best thing that you can do, when you have been left labeled as a single parent, is to move forward and be successful, regardless. You approach this the same way that we have decided to approach parenting, one day at a time.

Day 17, "Where's YOUR daddy"

Day 18, "NOT again"

We take three steps forward and four steps backwards. Every time it seems like things are turning around, life happens. You're finally able to stick to your budget, something goes wrong with the car. You're finally able to plan a girl's night out, the baby gets sick. If it isn't one thing, it's another. Doesn't it seem like life hates you sometimes? I have good news, it doesn't. It's not just you. It's life.

Life happens. This phrase could have filled up all 31 days of affirmation and meant something different every time. If by now the point of this book is still missing, I am here to let you know that it is all going to be okay. No matter how many "not again" moments arise, it is going to be okay. No matter how many curveballs life throws, it's going to be okay. "Why do you keep telling me this?" Because it is absolutely going to be okay. Perspective is everything. It is not what actually happens to you, it's how you look at it.  If you can look at the opportunity in situations, identify the solution as opposed to giving life to the problem and decide to overcome it, you will be okay.

Sometimes bad things happen. Other times, we are the cause but either way, things are going to be okay. Even if you don't believe it, it's an image that I challenge you to wear until you do. Your children are watching. They learn how to approach life by how they've seen us go through our highs and lows. That's a lot of pressure, isn't it? It is! Remember that the next time you are going through. Someone is watching you and learning how to deal with life by watching what you do.

Day 18, "NOT again"

Day 19, "Teens, how many of us have them"

Teenagers are crazy! There I said it! I meant it too! I heard a parent say that your real child is kidnapped during the teenage years and replaced with a pod. If you have had the pleasure of making it out of the teenage years, alive, God bless you! If you're like me and still navigating through the teenage years, God bless you! If you have not yet made it to the teenage years, RUN! Then when you return, God bless you! Our babies change. They know everything and nothing.

Want everything, appreciate nothing. Life is simple unless you're 16. If you are 16 you have experiences that no other person, especially an adult can ever fathom. Mom it's not just your teen that's crazy, they all are. It has absolutely nothing to do with you. Do you remember how great you were at 16? Me neither, because I wasn't. I was crazy too, but I like to think that my crazy made sense. If that even makes any sense. I have no advice for you, I am trying to make it through this journey too, but I can encourage you. This is the time in their lives where they need their mommy's the most. They need our understanding. They need our ears. They need our direction and rearing but most importantly, they need our trust. Our trust in ourselves, the foundations that we have set and that they listened to what we have done, then said, all of those years prior.

They must learn through discovery. As terrifying as that sounds, we must give them room to fail and be there to redirect them when they do.

Day 19, "Teens, how many of us have them"

Day 20, "Clean IT UP"

Fix it! The messes that you have made cannot go unresolved. The situations that were centered on you cannot linger. They don't correct themselves. You don't get to just walk away from issues, problems or people when the problem was you. You must close the loop on unhandled disputes and relationships. If you do not, you will find yourself dealing with these things again. The laws of reciprocity and karma do not change so you will sow what you reap. Why go through that? Being a good parent, adult and role model all have one

thing in common: accountability. Accountability is simply taking responsibility for things that have happened and accepting the outcomes or repercussions. Our children repeat what they see far more than they ever repeat what they hear. Mommy, you can't run from it. Clean it up! I would fail you if I allowed every day to read as though life is grand regardless of what you do. We do play a part in our struggles sometimes we are more so responsible than life, typically. Parenting is fluid. Being a woman is fluid. Being a human is fluid. There are no guides to being great at these. Great is a subjective adjective in all these situations. But we do have somewhat of an outline. There's a book that gives the basics and a few examples, called the bible. There are a few people that we know who we admire, God gives us examples. We don't have any excuse to not be the best that we can be. Our success and failure start with us. Our relationships are critical to our success. If you made a mess, clean it up!

Day 20, "Clean IT UP"

Day 21, "Where'd THAT mess come from"

Have you ever walked in the house and wanted to turn back around, walk back outside, get back in your car and pull off? Maybe you'd recheck the address and come back later because you were certain that your house could not possibly look like that. You had no idea where that mess could have possibly come from. As a matter of fact, you weren't even aware that you had that much stuff in your kitchen, living room, teen's room or nursery. That is life! Out of nowhere there'll be something. Are you the type of person who grabs the cleaning supplies and just starts fixing it or are you the one who takes a step back to identify how it started? We have a bad habit as mothers, we often want to just make it better. We don't typically take the time to discover, especially when it has to do with our kids, we just want to clean it up. Mommy, not everything is black and white. Not everything will disappear with Ajax. Sometimes we can't just fix it. We should always step back and identify why it happened in the first place. Until we address the root cause, we will never address the mess. We'll keep coming home, turning around, and walking back outside until we get to the bottom of why the house's being torn up in the first place.

Day 21, "Where'd THAT mess come from"

Day 22, "Because I said SO"

Every argument with a child has been won with, "Because I said so!" This is the conversation ender. The credits roll and the crowd leaves when a mother makes this statement. This declarative statement is the most dangerous one in the mommy arsenal. What it says is, I do not need any other reason. I don't need any support for what I am telling you to do. I don't have to model anything, do what I tell you to do.

More often than not, it's hypocritical. We expect our children to blindly follow this instruction then wonder why they will not question the words of others in their lives. As a matter of fact, we're typically furious if they tell us that they listened to someone else.

The glaring difference is that we're their mom, that's also our defense. We wouldn't do anything to hurt them or tell them anything wrong. Although that is true, there comes a time where they trust others like they trust us. There'll be a time when everything we say will be questioned while their peers will appear to be the gospel. This is one of the key reasons why our actions must align with our words. They will hear what we do far more often than they hear what we say. Our influence dims for a season and it is in that season that we will need them to rely on the root.

What have you shown your children that is contrary to what you have said?

Day 22, "Because I said SO"

Day 23, "I thank GOD for you"

If you have anyone in your life that acts a confidant, a shoulder, or an anchor, thank God for them daily! We know that being a parent can be a lonely road and it's simply unfair to burden your children with adult problems so they can't act as your friend. We all need someone to talk to, who'll keep our secrets, tell us the truth when we're wrong and that we trust. There won't be many of these people in our lives, but it is key that we have them. Preferably this is not the same person. As a mom, you know how burdensome it is to be everything for someone, we don't want to drain anyone else in our life in that

way. If it is one person, check on them to make sure that they can carry your burdens. Sometimes, out of consideration, you'll have to lighten the load and deal with things on your own to keep them from bearing too much of your weight. Are you one of these things for someone? Can someone lean on you? Trust you?

Can you have difficult conversations and tell someone when they're wrong? You're a mom. The answer should be yes. If our children can't trust us to always be honest with them, who can they trust? Integrity is a character trait and it starts with honesty. Allow your kids to see these types of healthy relationships. Be this type of healthy relationship and your child will mimic what they see you do as well as say. It's a great step towards healing what's broken in the world, one family at a time.

Day 23, "I thank GOD for you"

Day 24, "You bring me JOY"

Look in the mirror. Smile. Point and say, "You bring me joy!" Then hug yourself! When life gets out of control, repeat. When the kids are acting crazy, repeat. When you wake up on the wrong side of the bed for no apparent reason, repeat. It all starts and stops with you so even if it is a lie in the moment, repeat! As an individual, a mom, a woman, and a human, you must live the change you want to see.

You must embody the joy you want in your life. It all starts with a changed mind. You change your mind by what you feed yourself. Start telling yourself that you're happy. Start telling yourself that you're beautiful. Start telling yourself that you're successful. Start telling yourself that you're a great mom. What you tell yourself, you believe. What you believe, you enact. What you enact becomes habitual and soon a lifestyle. It is all about you. This entire 31 days is dedicated to you. Love you. Embrace you. Look at yourself and say, "You bring me joy!"

Day 24, "You bring me JOY"

Day 25, "WHAT fees"

Daycare! Graduation! Pictures! Athletics! What do these things have in common? They're all fees that you will have to pay over the tenure of your parenting. They're inevitable! They're expensive! They're technically mandatory! They're a part of your child's educational experience and major milestones that you may regret not capturing or participating in. There'll be ample items that come up in life that'll fit the characteristics of fees. Some you can prepare for, some unexpected but there will be items that arise which will fit this bill. What in your life is a fee that you can't afford to pay? We

are not talking about any of the aforementioned, we're talking about expenses that just aren't worth it. We're talking about costs that return no reward. We're talking about those things that just aren't necessary but are expensive. They're eating away at your peace of mind. They're charging interest to your time. They're constantly costing you something and you simply can't afford them anymore. Fees can be a person, place or thing. Bad habits or addictions. Identify these things and cut them loose. There'll be enough necessary sacrifices throughout the years. Let go of the things that return no benefits, don't make memories that hurt you more than help. Remove the unnecessary "fees" from your life!

Day 25, "WHAT fees"

Day 26, "THIS kid"

If you pay attention when your children talk, you will find yourself learning far more from them than you think they learn from you. Small children love unconditionally, befriend anyone without prejudice and are simply nice to people who are nice to them. Teens point out the inconsistencies in the world, analyze everything and can identify what's fair. Our children can make us have "ah ha" moments that we're sometimes ashamed to admit. While talking to my, then, 14-year-old about relationships she paraphrased a

situation that we both observed and simply said, "adults behave like children when they're in love. They are petty. Is this what I have to look forward to?" The only response that I could give her was, "Yes! Love brings out the immaturity in everyone and age has nothing to do with it." What is that thing that you do? What is that thing that you tell your child not to do, that you do? What is that thing that you know you have no business doing yet you still do? Are all three answers the same? If so, this will be simpler than I thought. Listen, we all have something. We have a level of immaturity, arrogance or insecurity that we struggle with. This thing comes out when we're hurt, ashamed or defeated. This thing is obvious to others regardless to how much we try to hide it. This thing is a part of us. Our kids see it. Whatever it is, identify it. Own it. Make a conscience effort to change it. Be the change you want to see or accept it when your children show you, you, through their actions.

Could you live with being on the receiving end of this thing?

Day 26, "THIS kid"

Day 27, "STOP crying"

It is not fair! Why did this happen to me? What am I going to do? We've all found ourselves either making this statement or asking these questions at some point in life. We may very well find ourselves repeating them again. What do you do next? Once you have identified the unfairness, wallowed in the wonder of "why me" and pondered your next step, what did you do? I hope your answer contained the extremely popular catch phrase," I put on my big girl panties…" There is not a problem that will ever be solved by crying.

You should absolutely express and address your emotions. Crying is therapeutic, it's just not an answer. Dry your tears. Blow your nose. Forgive others. Forgive yourself. Outline a plan of attack and get to work. In every situation there's a part that we played. Sometimes the hardest part of moving forward is failing to accept that and forgive ourselves. No one can do anything to you without your permission.

No action can be perpetuated habitually without your participation. Isolated incidents are just that, isolated, so that means we have moved on from it. Anything that constantly happens to us is voluntary. Mommy, we have work to do. We don't have time for negative patterns. We don't have time for repeat offenses. We don't have time for the same mistakes. We do not have time to be a victim. No more, "It's not fair! Why did this happen to me? What am I going to do? ".
Stop crying! It's time for a change.

Day 27, "STOP crying"

Day 28, "Give me ONE minute"

"Give me one minute, I'll be right out!" has been heard by every parent either early in the morning before school or when attempting to leave for somewhere you should have been earlier. Why is that? Why are we never ready on time? You may be reading this with a perplexed look because you are the most punctual person you know so you can't relate. I'm one of those people too so I'm with you but guess what, this isn't always about us and contrary to how much we try to control the situation, we'll find ourselves needing more time. The need may not be caused by a child running late. It may not be

caused by uncontrollable traffic. We did everything right, planned accordingly and provided our self with wiggle room but regardless to our preparation, we still needed more time. Mommy, this is yet another time that I ask you to be patient with you. We have agreed that life will happen. We have agreed that we'll cause things to go left in life ourselves. We have also agreed that our perception dictates the outcome. Here is when all those things must be applied. When you've auto paid the rent and there's a last-minute emergency, you find yourself needing more time. When you've scheduled an outing, but a hair appointment ran late, you'll find yourself needing more time. When you've planned a vacation, but a work assignment cannot wait until you return, you need more time.

These are situations outside of our control. These are situations that are influenced by others yet affect us. These are the nuances of life and no matter how frustrated you become, take a deep breath and allow yourself, more time.

Day 28, "Give me ONE minute"

Day 29, "NO"

Say it with me, "NO!" One more time, "NO!" Now say it like you meant it, "NO!" I want you to practice this, practice it often because you should say it as necessary and mean it when you do. As mommy's we have the tendency to act as the end all, be all. We want to do everything for everyone whenever we're asked. We assume that our ability to do is an indication of how much we love our family. We burn ourselves out. We beat ourselves up. We neglect ourselves. We run ourselves into the ground and don't realize it until we're so emotionally worn that we're ready to snap. In some cases, we don't realize it until the actual outburst happens. By then, it's too late. This could have been avoided if we said how we felt. No, I can't do this, this, that or the other. No, I don't have time to take you there. Your inability to do does not

make you a bad mom. Sometimes, things must be rescheduled or missed. You will always do what you can, when you can and that will always be appreciated, so, why do you believe that the world will end if you can't? Sure, it's just you mommy. I get that. It's tremendous pressure but it is okay to not do everything, all the time and in one day. Be kind to yourself. Plan responsibly. Communicate to the children and do what you can when you can. For the things that you cannot, say, "NO!"

Day 29, "NO"

Day 30, "YES Ma"

Music to my ears, "Yes Ma!" Have you cleaned your room? Yes Ma! Have you finished studying? Yes Ma! Have you graduated from college with a 4.0 and applied to Grad School? Yes Ma! Well that last one is a dream but not impossible and it is just one of those many examples of where we love to hear, "Yes Ma!" From toddler to marriage, we will never get tired of hearing our children tell us yes as confirmation of completion. It's an expectation when we ask the question. It's somewhat of a setup. We never really ask them questions without some indication of what the answer will be.

Moms are slick in that way. Why is that? Why do we ask our children questions that we know the answer to? What happens if they say, "No Ma!" or anything contrary to our expectation? What will we do? What have you done? I know it's happened. It's happened to us all. They've disappointed us in some form and fashion by not performing to our expectation. Do we love them any less? Do we treat them any different? Are we not their mother anymore? Sounds sort of crazy when you read these questions in this context, doesn't it? It does. So why do you beat yourself up when you fall short? Why do you play it safe?

Ask yourself, answer yourself and work on yourself.
It is going to be okay, mommy!

Day 30, "YES Ma"

Day 31, "It's TOO quiet"

Moms, what is our first response when there is a missing toddler and silence? Do you run through the house in anticipation of a mess? Do you start yelling through the house in hopes that a small person will say, "Hmm?" It's a natural motherly instinct to be afraid of silence. In a mom's world, if there's silence, there's a problem. When they're teens, you find yourself seeking the peace and quiet. You are content with everyone being in their neutral corner, on their devices, not fighting. You embrace those moments. When they're grown and gone, you're excited about the silence for a moment then you look for noise. You try to fill your time and space with activity because you miss those days of the skeptical quiet, the peaceful, distracted quiet, etc.

Why can't we be content in whatever state we are in? When they're babies, we can't wait until they can walk. When they're toddlers, we can't wait until they're school age. When they're school age, we can't wait until they're teens. When they're teens, we can't wait until they leave. We spend so much time concerned about what's next, we can't relish in where we are. At the close of these 31 days, I want you to do a few things for me: 1. Be okay! 2. Love yourself! 3. Remain positive! And 4. Enjoy the moment!

We are writing the "Great" mom handbook as we go, for our families and sharing tidbits on the way.

While authoring, the greatest parts of the story are the moments. Enjoy them, be okay with the quiet, in whatever stage it's in.

Day 31, "It's TOO quiet"

www.ingramcontent.com/pod-product-compliance
Lightning Source LLC
Chambersburg PA
CBHW062114290426
44110CB00023B/2805